Outsourcing: The Competitive Advantages

By Ade Asefeso MCIPS MBA

Second Edition

ISBN-13: 978-1499649802

ISBN-10: 1499649800

Publisher: AA Global Sourcing Ltd
Website: http://www.aaglobalsourcing.com

Table of Contents

Disclaimer

This publication is designed to provide competent and reliable information regarding the subject matter covered. However, it is sold with the understanding that the author and publisher are not engaged in rendering professional advice. The authors and publishers specifically disclaim any liability that is incurred from the use or application of contents of this book.

If you purchased this book without a cover you should be aware that this book may have been stolen property and reported as "unsold and destroyed" to the publisher. In this case neither the author nor the publisher has received any payment for this "stripped book."

Dedication

This book is dedicated to the hundreds of thousands of incredible souls in the world who have weathered through the up and down of recent recession.

To my family and friends who seems to have been sent here to teach me something about who I am supposed to be. They have nurtured me, challenged me, and even opposed me…. But at every juncture has taught me!

This book is dedicated to my lovely boys, Thomas, Michael and Karl. Teaching them to manage their finance will give them the lives they deserve. They have taught me more about life, presence, and energy management than anything I have done in my life.

Chapter 1: What is Business Outsourcing?

Companies might consider business outsourcing for many different reasons. Outsourcing might be considered for many different business segments.

Business outsourcing is when a company hires an outside source to complete work or a project which would normally be done by the staff.

A company might consider outsourcing for saving money by cutting down on costs or they might not have the employee resources to complete a particular project.

Outsourcing gives a company the opportunity to complete a needed project performed by people who are not their employees.

This means they do not have to pay a salary or provide benefits to the people also.

When business outsourcing occurs the company will usually enter into an agreement with the outsourcing company which is usually a contract.

The contract will usually include the terms of the agreement like steps throughout the project, time the project will take, people involved, cost, and required resources from the client.

There are many different types of outsourcing.

Examples of a segment of business that hires outsourcing companies for assistance include UK and US manufacturing companies looking for help with payroll, logistic and production etc.

The biggest field of outsourcing today for companies is in the Information Technology field. This is because companies will upgrade their phones, computers, need cabling installed, troubleshooting, and more.

Companies also outsource people for customer service positions, call centres, and telemarketing.

Outsourcing is a solution for a business to save money and complete projects and tasks in the workforce without having full time employees do the work.

Outsourcing is becoming more and more popular across the world every day.

Chapter 2: A Blast from the Past: The History of Outsourcing

Outsourcing has become a common term used in businesses - big or small. It is the process of hiring organizations to do specific functions for a certain company. Most often than not, most of the outsourced jobs are those that are not directly related to the core of the business activities.

Rather, the functions are those that can be considered as non-core business activities or those that are not related to the main business but are somehow quite necessary for businesses in general.

Outsourcing, as it has been proven for the past few years, has become an essential part of businesses. Companies from all over the globe practice it but how many really know what the history of outsourcing is.

Just like with any other things, outsourcing too has a beginning. To be able to appreciate what outsourcing really is, a quick look at its history is necessary.

The Roots

It has been said that outsourcing started ever since people began producing and selling items such as tools, food, and household items. As society and communities grew, people began to do specialized works and traded with other people goods for services and vice versa. Looking at it, it can be said that people a thousand years ago were already practicing a form of outsourcing.

When the industrial age came between the years 1800s to 1900s, companies were vertically integrated and did not practice outsourcing. Each company took care of everything from production to manufacturing to deliveries. Companies in these eras handled their own payrolls, taxes, and hired their own lawyers. Everything was an internal affair. This kind of setup however does not encompass all organizations at that time but this was the trend at that time.

As time passed by, specialization contracting gained popularity especially in the field of service industry. This was the beginning of the modern outsourcing practice. During the industrial revolution, services such as insurance, engineering and architecture have begun to be outsourced to 3rd part organizations although the client company and the specialized organization usually just belong to the same area or country.

The Beginnings of Offshore Outsourcing

Onshore outsourcing was growing to be more and more productive for businesses. It all started out with outsourcing low-valued items such as apparels and toys and transcended to outsourcing items with higher values such as appliances and other electronic gadgets. In the history of outsourcing, it was manufacturing that first left the main land to offshore destinations. This move by businesses was for the chance to save on costs.

At first, offshore outsourcing garnered a few apprehensions from business proprietors. But with the improvement of logistics, offshore outsourcing gained popularity. With the development in education and skills of lower wage countries, the value of offshore outsourcing became higher. In fact, during the 1970s, computer related manufacturing was also outsourced offshore. The process of outsourcing just grew and has never stopped since.

Today, outsourcing different functions has never been easier with the help of the information technology. Data can easily be sent and received through the information superhighway. It is not uncommon to see in your daily items such as in the R & D of your prescription drugs that they are outsourced to companies in other countries.

Chapter 3: Outsourcing: Why and how to Outsource your Business

Outsourcing is one of the latest buzzwords in the business world. It is an effective business solution that will truly benefit any company. Outsourcing means you will be hiring a third party company to do your company's business or at least part of it. So, why outsource your business when you can do the business of your company in-house?

The main reason why companies today are outsourcing their business or at least part of their business to other companies is that it is relatively cheaper than doing it in-house. For example, if your company needs a customer care department or a help desk, you will need a particularly large office space for this department and a lot of materials, such as computers, software and your company will also hire a large amount of manpower to act as call centre agents or help desk agents.

If you outsource it to call centre companies, you will definitely not need to hire additional employees and you will not need to purchase the technology needed to run an effective call centre department. You will also not need to devote an office space as the office can be in another country.

Companies prefer outsourcing in another country or offshore outsourcing, particularly in developing countries, such as India, Philippines, China, and countries in Latin America. This is because there is quite a large pool of talented individuals joining the workforce every year in these countries. Qualified and talented professionals in these countries can provide the same quality services as the qualified individuals in developed countries with companies that outsource their business or part of it, such as the United States, Canada, and countries in Europe.

This means that the companies who outsource their business in developing countries have access to cheap labour. They can save as much as half of their budget when they do not outsource or when they perform their businesses in-house.

Another reason is that the companies who outsource their business or part of their business will be able to focus more in the development of their company. Companies will be able to make full use of their facilities and resources for other important matters to make the company grow or improve.

The office space intended for the outsourced job can be used for another department. It can be an expansion of another department or it can be an entirely new department that the company may add.

Finding the right company to outsource your business can be rather easy to do. You actually don't have to travel to the country where you plan on outsourcing your business. All you have to do is search for it in your favourite search engine in the internet and you can expect a lot of results.

Since there are a lot of companies that offer outsourcing services, there will be a great chance that you will find a company that will suit your company's needs. It is recommended however that you should look for a company that is known to provide quality outsourced work. Find out if the company have ever worked with the same business you have in order to know that the company you plan on hiring have an experience in your field before.

Remember these things and you will know why outsourcing can definitely help your business and where and how to find the right company to get your business outsourced.

Chapter 4: Offshore Outsourcing Services: What is it and what can you get from It?

First of all, you have to understand what offshore outsourcing services really imply. Offshore outsourcing means that a company will be hiring another company to work on their business processes. The company that offers offshore outsourcing services will be doing the business process or part of the business process.

Companies in developed countries, such as the United States, Canada, and European nations are now outsourcing their business process or part of their business process in order to save money. This is the primary reason why companies today are now outsourcing their business processes.

Companies that offer outsourcing services are usually offshore or are located in other countries. Usually, countries from developing nations do this because of the high demand for outsourcing services from western countries.

If you have a company, then outsourcing can be one of the best things that can happen to your business, in case you choose to outsource your business process to offshore companies. Besides, because you can save your company from spending a lot of money and at the same time fully function as a whole company, who wouldn't want to get outsourcing services from offshore companies?

By outsourcing, your company will be able to save significant amounts of money. This is because offshore companies, particularly in developing nations, charges only a fraction of the amount to get the job done compared to your own country. Developing nations that usually offers outsourcing services are China, the Philippines, Mexico, and India. These countries are considered to have such a low labour cost that companies from developed countries are considering hiring their services to get their business process work done.

Another benefit of outsourcing for your company is that it can take heavy workloads off and divide it to offshore companies to do part of your company's workload. Because of this, your company will be able to focus on more important matters to make your company more competitive in the world of business.

If you are in the software developing business, it is better that you should outsource part of your software development department in order to cut operational costs and at the same time, let your in-house software development department breathe.

This is because IT professionals in developed countries, such as in the United States charge a high amount of fee for every software developed. If you outsource it to offshore companies, particularly in developing countries, such as India, and the Philippines, that has a large pool of qualified and equally talented IT professionals, they will charge you for only a fraction of the amount that IT professionals will charge you in your own country.

For example, if a programming job costs about 100 dollars in your country and the same programming job in offshore countries cost only 20 dollars to develop, you would want to hire the cheaper alternative. Obviously, if you need 100 or 200 of these programming jobs, you can see the difference in cost. Your company will be able to save thousands of dollars if you offshore your business process or part of your business process.

Always remember that you only have to offshore certain jobs. You should never offshore any projects regarding strategies of your business. You should also consider the quality of the product the offshore company can provide. If the offshore company's product is not at par with your company's standards, you should not hire the company at all. You better look for an offshore company that provides better quality.

Chapter 5: Top Six Benefits of Business Outsourcing

Small businesses can benefit from business outsourcing. Rather focusing exclusively on the costs of outsourcing certain activities of your business, you should also consider the benefits such a change would bring.

Cost Reduction Business outsourcing can help lower your business's expenses. Let's say you have clothing business. The equipment you are using is not the best in the line, and it contributes to increasing your production costs. But what if you simply outsource your equipment needs instead? Would you be able to lower your production costs?

Labour costs can be reduced as well. Rather than hiring temporary or project-based employees, why not simply outsource your human resource needs to BPO vendors who know exactly what they are doing? Working with an experienced firm will ensure that you do not have to waste time going through dozens of applicants just to find a perfect fit.

No Waste of Time Business outsourcing let you take on projects right away and start on them immediately. Rather than spending time amassing your resources, you can simply approach a BPO vendor and they will provide you with all the resources you need for a fixed cost. The BPO vendor will take care of everything, from screening applicants to training them for their new job. All you need to do is simply give the BPO vendor an idea of what your needs are.

Improved Efficiency Consider how your business operates. Is marketing research and development or product distribution slowing you down? If none of them make up your company's core competencies then nothing is stopping you from outsourcing them. By contracting such functions to a trusted third party, your company's efficiency is improved two-fold: you have more time to focus on more important activities while contracted activities are performed at an even more efficient rate since they have greater resources and expertise than you do in those fields.

Act Big Small businesses are David and the big scary corporations are Goliath. But David managed to beat Goliath, didn't he? And all he had was a sling. In the world of business, BPO vendors are the ones that could provide you with the exact kind of sling you need to defeat your competitors. With the help of business outsourcing, you will be able to level the playing field and maybe even face down the competition in time.

Lower Risk Almost everything in business comes with a certain degree of risk. Of course, the lower the risk, the better your position is. Business outsourcing can reduce the risk you are taking in various ways. When you are entering a new market, you can let a local BPO firm handle marketing research and development for you and you will be privy to insider's knowledge.

Building Your Reputation You have graduated from a culinary school with flying honours and you bake the best brownies in town. You want to go into business but you do not know how to package and distribute your product effectively. Rather than force your customers to tolerate your bungling efforts, why not outsource your needs to a firm with the kind of expertise that will impress your customers?

By outsourcing your needs to experts, you are able to quickly build a name for yourself and be known not just for having the best brownies but ones that come in an excellent package, too!

These are not the only benefits of business outsourcing, but they will more than do for a start, don't they?

Chapter 6: Globalization through Outsourcing Trends

The relocation in managing the day-to-day carrying out of business activities or the enterprise's function to a peripheral service provider is being utilized today. The client organization and the supplier of services drafts and executes a contractual agreement that stipulates the rules and describes the terms of provision and procurement. Nowadays, outsourcing trends have become more expansive encompassing more and more industries. Offshore outsourcing is the transfer of the enterprise's service module to a secondary management that is located elsewhere other than the country where the goods and services are actually availed or consumed. The principle behind the practice is for minimization of production cost with the global electronic internet network as its enabling medium.

Primarily, the reason for engaging this method is due to a significant difference in salary allocation. It is expected that the cost of service in the host country is much lesser in comparison to that of the origin. General criteria for the job that may be sent overseas are jobs accomplished through telework, jobs with high information content, jobs that can be repeated and easy to set-up and work that could be transmitted through the internet.

However, this trend has been a source of controversy. Opposing factions have raised the threat it poses to the domestic job market of the developed country since fewer opportunities will be offered. Contrary to that, job opportunities in the host country will dramatically increase.

Cannibalization is yet another trend in outsourcing. It is characterized by the reclamation of the serviceable parts of the projects by which open production and failure-related requirements are executed with the use the existing components of the project. This practice ensures the efficacy and proficiency of the supportive facility.

In this case, the work done earlier which was proven to be unsuccessful is outsourced to someone who is basically home bound. The service provider may actually be situated in the same country as the organization in need of the output.

Growth in captives and organizations that are owned and operated by a parent firm but in a different country is also a way of outsourcing. Nationals of the parent firm who have transferred due to work or those who have been living in the place as expatriates compose workforce. A big part of the wage revenue basically goes to the country of origin since foreign citizens do not supply it.

Outsourced electronic commerce is yet another common trend wherein transactions for selling or buying a good or commodity is done over electronic systems. This has also gained popularity over the recent years. Since the development of the internet a significant increase in this area has been reported. The variety of business conducted through this process includes fund transfer, internet marketing, supply chain management, electronic data interchange, online transaction exchange, and several others.

The above-mentioned outsourcing trends have given the business sector a boost. Companies making use of these systems are generally more financially stable than those who do not. The face of business has been altered through globalization and de-regulation.

Chapter 7: When Outsourcing is the Only Option

Deciding whether or not to outsource particular tasks is one of the many important decisions both large and small companies alike have to make often. This can be a difficult decision at times but often the decision making process is greatly simplified and it becomes clear that outsourcing is the only viable option. Situations in which this may occur are when the in-house staff is not qualified for these tasks, when the in-house staff is already overburdened and when there are specific client requirements specifying certain tasks must be completed by individuals with specific qualifications. This book will address each of these situations and discuss why outsourcing becomes the only solution in each case.

The Qualification of in-house Staff

Sometimes outsourcing becomes the only option available because there are no in-house staff members qualified to perform a particular task. This often occurs when a task requires a highly specialized degree or area of expertise. This is especially problematic when the task in question is one which is extremely rare. When this is the case it does not make sense for a company to hire an employee with these capabilities when they will be rarely utilized because employees who are not productive are expensive to the company. However, if this task becomes one which is required regularly, the question of whether or not to outsource the task becomes more complicated. As this book is focusing on situations where outsourcing is the only option, we will not delve further into the factors which complicated this decision such as labour costs and increased manpower.

Smaller companies often face the problem of not having staff members qualified for particular tasks more often than larger companies. Larger companies obviously have a larger pool of employees to pull from and it is therefore much more likely for the smaller firms to have gaps in their level of expertise than it is for larger companies to have these gaps.

The Availability of in-house Staff

Sometimes outsourcing becomes the only option based on staff availability. A company may have a need for tasks to be completed rather quickly. Although it may be a task for which several in-house employees are qualified, current workloads may make it impossible for these employees to take on these tasks. When this occurs, outsourcing again becomes the only option. Company employees are often multitasking and may be working towards several serious deadlines at any one particular time. Management is tasked with the responsibility of doling out work to lower level employees and when they feel as though their in-house staff is not able to take on more work, they often turn to outsourcing as a solution.

Workloads often become a factor in outsourcing when there are projects which are particularly time sensitive in nature. Employees and employers often have to prioritize the multiple tasks they are managing but there are times when a number of projects or tasks become urgent simultaneously and when this happens it may become difficult to complete all of these tasks with only the assistance of the in-house staff.

Client Requirements

Sometimes outsourcing becomes the only option as a result of client requirements. Depending on the complexity of a task, a client may require the consultant firm tasked with completing a task to have the task performed by an individual with specific qualifications. These qualifications may include specific training in certain types of software, exact education requirements or previous work experiences. Companies who do not have in-house employees who meet these specific requirements have no choice but to outsource the task to a qualified individual.

When this is an isolated incident, companies often outsource the task and do not make efforts to attempt to hire a full time employee with these qualifications. This is a wise decision especially when the client requirements require an expert in a particular niche of the software industry. Employing an employee of this calibre would likely be rather expensive especially if he would rarely be called upon to utilize his advanced skills.

33

Chapter 8: Offshore Outsourcing: Finding the Right Country to Outsource your Company's Projects

Today, companies are now hiring other companies in other countries to do their business or part of their business. This particular type of business strategy is called offshore outsourcing.

It is a fact that in today's business world, offshore outsourcing is now becoming a very feasible trend for companies who wants to expand their business or to simply reduce their overhead expenses.

As an entrepreneur, you would definitely want to reduce the operating costs of your business without sacrificing your businesses functionality. By outsourcing your business or at least part of your business, you can indeed expand and reduce operating expenses. Outsourcing is a very large industry in developing countries, such as China, India and the Philippines. Your company can definitely hire companies in these three countries to outsource part of your business or even all of it. However, you should take note that you should choose an outsourcing company that provides quality and professionally done jobs.

You should also consider which country you should outsource your business in. People in different countries have different culture and education. You have to choose which people, culture, and educational standards that your company can benefit from.

For example, in India, this country has one of the largest populations of IT professionals in the world. Because of the British influenced educational systems in this country, the education on math and science in this country is greatly emphasized. This country has more than one hundred and twenty thousand trained IT professionals added to the workforce every year.

India is now being considered as an IT centre in developing countries and is also one of the countries that United States and British companies prefer for software or IT outsourcing. India has created a strong reputation as one of the leading countries in IT outsourcing industry in the world.

In the Philippines, it is an entirely different story. Because this nation is considered as Asia's English speaking countries that have 94% literacy rate, this country is also considered to have a large population of IT professionals in the world. With over three million college graduates joining the workforce every year, this country is indeed one of the best source for talent.

Although the Filipinos are Asian, it was influenced by Americans for over 50 years and has developed a western culture. Filipinos loves watching American television and because of this, the people in the Philippines are fluent in American English and can communicate effectively with Americans and other

English speaking nations.

Because the Filipinos are fluent in American English, this country have become a premier choice of the United States for call centre outsourcing. If you are looking for call centre services that are able to provide quality customer support service, the Philippines is definitely the country to look for call centres. Although India charges less for its call centre services than in the Philippines, more companies in the United States prefer the Philippines more for customer care jobs because of the quality of work they offer.

Another factor that the Philippines is chosen for call centre jobs is that not only that the people there speak fluent American English, but they are also friendly and helpful in nature.

These are the things you should consider when choosing a country to outsource your business or at least part of your business. You also have to consider the people living in it and the culture they were brought up with in order to know where to outsource your company's project.

Chapter 9: Reasons you Might Consider Business Outsourcing

There are many reasons you might consider outsourcing for your company. Many of those reasons might include the resources, cost, or staff.

If you are a growing company you might have many projects you need to complete for your expansion. If you are upgrading systems you might have projects you need to complete.

You might not have a staff that knows how to complete the project or your staff may not have enough people to complete the project in the time frame you would like it to be done.

Outsourcing is an excellent idea when you face issues like this. A company can come into your business and complete the project on your required deadline.

Another reason you might consider outsourcing is to save money. You might currently have full-time employees in positions that only require them to be around for certain times of the year.

It is cheaper to eliminate the full time employee position and bring in the outsourcing company only when you need them to work.

When you bring in an outsourcing company to complete a project rather than hire a full time employee you are saving on the yearly salary and the benefits you would have to offer that employee.

In most cases, it is usually cheaper to hire an individual or team of people on a temporary basis than to use your own staff.

There are many reasons you might consider outsourcing.

You might have a full-time employee you need for one specific thing but often has a lot of downtime and you have to find work for them to do to keep them busy.

There is no reason to pay a full-time employee if you can hire someone for the duration you need them.

Chapter 10: Offshore Call Centre Outsourcing: Economical Solution for Businesses

Thanks to the advancement in communication technology, it enabled business to save a lot of money on call centres. Companies today are now taking advantage of call centres and are now considering it as one of the most economical solutions for businesses.

Firstly, call centres manages tasks to satisfy customers, and attract customers for your company. Call centres can also be help desk support and advice centre for your business and it can handle both inbound and outbound calls for your company.

As you can see, call centres are a very important tool for businesses today in terms of customer relations. It is considered to be an essential part of any company in order to satisfy, attract and in keeping contact with your clients. However, it is also a fact that putting up your own call centre for your company can be very costly. It will require you to purchase the technology needed for it, such as computers, software, and it will also require you to hire additional employees to act as call centre agents.

This is why companies today are now considering hiring call centres offshore. If your company needs a call centre, you can outsource your call centre in other countries in order to cut some operational costs. Outsourcing your call centres in other countries, particularly developing countries, is very cheap because of the difference in the minimum salary rates with a particular developing country. You will see that the minimum wage is far lower than in your country.

Your company should prefer an offshore call centre that hires staff with good English speaking skills in order to communicate with your clients better. Developing countries, such as China, Philippines and India are three of the most popular countries that provide great quality services for a call centre. They have a lot of talented individuals with great English skills that will be able to communicate effectively with your customers.

When you are outsourcing your call centre offshore, it is important to consider the following things before you sign the contract in order to ensure quality service:

• English proficiency – The call centre agents in the offshore call centre should be able to have good English speaking skills. They should be able to communicate with your clients well in order to satisfy their inquiries. This is very important because call centres are supposed to be the communication ties between your client and your company.

• Average call waiting time – It is also important that you should find out how much your client will have to wait until their calls are taken by the call centre agent. It is important to realize that there will be clients who will be complaining about your products and services and you should realize that they are already irate before they even made the call. Making them wait will only add to their dissatisfaction and irritability. This is why it is important that a call centre should be able to take your client's call as soon as possible.

• Length of conversation – The call centre agent should be able to handle the calls as short as possible. They should provide the best answer possible in order to satisfy your clients as soon as possible and make the call as short as possible. By doing this, the call centre will be able to handle more calls.

These are some of the features that you should look for in a call centre. This is why it is important for you or your staff to call the call centre and pose as a client in order to know about the quality of their work and also make sure that it isn't deteriorating.

Chapter 11: Why Companies Today are Outsourcing their Jobs to Foreign Countries

Outsourcing is the latest buzzword in the business world today. Because of outsourcing, companies today are becoming more competitive and more efficient in doing their businesses. So, what is it about outsourcing that it is so hot in today's business world?

First of all, you need to know about outsourcing before rushing in to call other companies and outsource your business process. Outsourcing is a method that a company does by hiring other companies to do the other company's business process or at least part of the business process in order to save a lot of money and allow the company to concentrate its resources to more important matters.

This is why outsourcing is so popular in the business world today. With outsourcing, you will now able to save your company from spending a lot of money and at the same time, make your company concentrate on more important matters.

Usually, companies outsource their business process to other companies that accepts outsourced jobs in foreign countries. Companies today prefer outsourcing in developing countries, such as Mexico, Philippines, China and India because of the relatively cheap labour in these countries offer.

For example, if your company needs a help desk department in order for your clients to reach your company to get their questions answered regarding the products and services they purchased from you, your company will spend a lot of money in creating this department. You will need to purchase computers, get it on a network, purchase help desk software and also hire additional employees to act as help desk representatives. Not only that, you will also devote a significantly large office space in order to accommodate the help desk department. Also, the employees you hire will be asking you for a high salary with full company benefits as a full time employee.

Now that you see how costly it is to create and maintain a help desk department, you should consider outsourcing it to save a lot of money and at the same time, save office space that you can later use for more important company matters.

Outsourcing to foreign countries that has call centres will enable you to cut on operational costs. They will charge you for their services but it will be significantly lower than maintaining your own in-house help desk.

You have to realize how much money you can save if you outsource.

Another vital factor is that your company will be able to divide the business process and let your company concentrate on more important matters, such as marketing, looking for new clients and other money making ventures that your company should prioritize.

The key feature in outsourcing your jobs to foreign countries that charge less is very obvious. With outsourcing, you will be able to save on company expenditures and at the same time, make your company competitive once again in the business world.

However, you should always remember that you should make sure that the company you will be outsourcing your company's job in should produce a high quality product. In call centres, you should look for a company that employs people who speaks fluent English with little or no hint that they are from foreign countries and speaks English only as their second language.

So, if you think that you need your company to be more efficient, competitive and save a lot of money, you should consider outsourcing your company's jobs or part of your company's job in foreign countries.

Chapter 12: Taking a Good Look at the Growth of Outsourcing

The definition of outsourcing is to assign certain functions or processes of a business to a 3rd party organization that provides services related to that specific function. This is done by the virtue of an agreement manifested by a contract that indicates the terms of services which includes the scope and limitations. In this contract, the service provider gets to make use of the resources of the client company while the client company acquires the services from the provider company.

The history of outsourcing goes a long a way back. Modern outsourcing started with manufacturing outsourcing which in the past involved big company names such as Coca-Cola. It outsourced supply chains so that they may be able to have more time to focus on the marketing aspect of the business. From this simple beginning, outsourcing has gone a long way since then.

Today, Business Process Outsourcing is growing at an enormous rate. It encompasses back office functions being outsourced offshore. These functions include HR management services and accounting services.

These past few decades, outsourcing has gone through a lot of changes. From doing simple tasks and functions, service providers nowadays are given more serious and critical jobs related to the company.

What used to be considered as a dreaded area to tread into, companies have become fond of offshore outsourcing instead of onshore outsourcing which proved to be more beneficial in terms of the relationship between money and quality. In offshore outsourcing, it has been observed that results yielded are of good quality but obtained at a lower cost.

The Boom of the Outsourcing Industry

The rapid growth of the outsourcing industry would have not been possible if not for the rise of the Internet. The increase in Internet users has contributed so much in this industry. The boundaries that separated one nation from the other have been severed by the information superhighway thus making it easier for people to communicate with each other. A person from one side of the world can easily communicate with another person at the opposite side of the planet as if they are just next door neighbours.

With the whole world being wired together, it was very easy to transport jobs to people outside the main nation. And with the advantage of the difference in time zones, tasks and functions can be done on a 24-hour basis when outsourcing.

The Benefits of Outsourcing

1) One of the most important benefits of outsourcing is cost savings. By tapping into the lower cost economies, companies in industrialized nations can take advantage of the developing nations.

2) Outsourcing vendors are usually fee-for-service basis. This means that they are only paid when certain jobs or functions are done. This scheme is very beneficial for companies.

3) Companies become more flexible when it comes to making use of their resources especially in times of cyclical fluctuations.

4) The client company can focus and give more time to the core business activities. The burden of carrying other non-core functions will be handled by other 3rd party service providers.

5) Business process will be speed-up due to the fact that certain functions will be taken care of specialists in that area. It is also not just about speed but with quality of work as well.

6) Errors and mistakes can easily be detected and can easily be fixed.

Given these benefits, the outsourcing industry will continue to grow in the future as major parts of businesses.

Chapter 13: Models of Offshore Outsourcing

Offshore outsourcing is simply defined as outsourcing to outside countries. Some people may think that the process of offshore outsourcing is a walk in the park producing large sums of profits. This notion however is erroneous. It takes a lot of work and initiative to make offshore outsourcing work and produce desirable results. It involves choosing the right model of offshore outsourcing that would fit a particular business need or situation.

Choosing the right model of offshore outsourcing is a very critical phase that companies undergo. Any decision made can either make or break their business options offshore. Making the decision on what model to choose involves aspect of selecting which country, economic conditions of a country, international business strategy, and outsourcing strategy.

There are currently three models of offshore outsourcing that are popular among businesses. These three are outsourcing to a service provider, joint ventures and subsidiaries.

Outsourcing to a Service Provider

Outsourcing to a service provider is the most evident offshore outsourcing model. It has a lot of coverage that range from small projects to multi-year contracts that amount to millions of dollars.

The simplest form of outsourcing to a service provider is onsite subcontracting. In this form, a company assigns its skilled personnel directly at the client's site. The people assigned will then become part of the client's team. This form of offshore outsourcing is perhaps the simplest and is commonly used by small organizations that are tied with the client company.

Another form of outsourcing a service provider is pure offshore projects. In this form, the scope of the functions is properly defined and work can be done remotely that requires little to no supervision. A good example of this is assigning work to small organizations or even to individuals, freelancers as they are commonly called. With the help of online tools, projects can easily be sent and received by hired firms or individuals all over the world.

Offshore outsourcing individual projects is another form wherein a certain function is subdivided into smaller chunks to be outsourced to vendor companies. This is usually assigned to vendors with whom the company has close ties with.

Joint Venture Offshore Model

In this model of offshore outsourcing, one organization establishes a relationship with a local company wherein both companies contribute to their resources. The main purpose of this goal is "I lend you my strength and you lend me yours." This creates a win-win situation wherein both companies can gain something from the tie up. With this kind of setup, the client organization will be able to minimize the risks of offshore outsourcing while on the other hand the local firm is given the opportunity to work with a large company scaling up their value chain.

The joint venture offshore model is sometimes considered as the stepping stone of the client organization to move on to the next offshore outsourcing model which is the subsidiary offshore model.

Subsidiary Offshore Model

From the joint venture model, a company may transcend to the subsidiary offshore model. However, it is also possible for the client company to move directly with the subsidiary offshore model without passing through the joint venture model given that they have enough confidence and are comfortable with tackling the local market. The most challenging part in this kind of offshore outsourcing model is the general management of the onsite units especially the staff.

To rap-up this chapter, offshore outsourcing is not as easy as some people may think it is. It needs thorough planning as well as making the right decisions. This includes choosing the right offshore outsourcing model that your company needs. It is even possible that a hybridization of the models is needed just to suit the needs of your organization. So plan well and choose well.

Chapter 14: Business Process Outsourcing – Bpo 2.0

Not that many experts think that business process outsourcing has a bright future. But despite the bad looks that BPO has been given, this industry continues to grow bigger and bigger. It may seem like a phenomenal event but taking a closer look, you will realize that its growth is due to the hard work of the people in the BPO industry.

Compared to other industries, people in the BPO have anticipated the challenges and emerging trends earlier making it possible to create new innovative strategies that largely contribute to its survival and amazing growth.

Although the future for this industry looks promising, there is no time for taking quick rests since the environment for this kind of business is rapidly changing. This is due to the fact that newer concepts and technologies are being developed.

These are also the reasons why the BPO industry is regularly checking out for new service delivery systems and customer management to keep up with the fast growing pace as well as satisfy the clients" expectations. With the constant perseverance of the people in the BPO industry, they have achieved this goal and as evidence there is now what is called BPO 2.0.

BPO 2.0

BPO 2.0 was developed for the satisfaction of customers. This system has succeeded where other industries have failed. It focuses on the utilization of advanced technologies that are cost-effective. With the deployment of BPO 2.0, the BPO industry in India has achieved the goals of the system which is reducing operational costs and improving quality as well as efficiency.

These two objectives are very important since customers are becoming more demanding and will not be satisfied with mediocrity customer services. Also, reducing costs have become a big issue because of the rising competition in the BPO industry and because companies are starting to reduce the budget for outsourcing. This is the reason why outsourcing hubs in India are forced to reduce cost expenditures.

For now BPO 2.0 has been implemented mostly to call centres industry in India but given the benefits that this new scheme can give to other outsourcing industries, it is not impossible to assume that they may follow suit in the future – implementing the BPO 2.0 methodologies and schemes.

But before this could happen, other outsourcing industries should re-evaluate their existing strategies. Also, it is important for the companies to prepare themselves for any possible changes that might occur when implementing BPO 2.0. This will affect the infrastructure of the company which in turn would require increased participation of available human resources so as to be able to support the new inputs as well as the advanced technologies under BPO 2.0.

The future of the business process outsourcing industry is quite bright. But this does not mean that challenges and hurdles along the way do not exist. One thing is for sure though and that is BPO 2.0 will stay because of the fact that it is a comprehensive service delivery system and customer management. This is good news for companies that have implemented BPO 2.0 and to those who are in the process of shifting.

For those who still have apprehensions with the business process industry. Statistics and facts will tell you that the BPO industry indeed is still on the rise and will continue to do so in the future.

Chapter 15: Your Job Just Got Easier with Outsourcing

If you are like most Internet marketers you often find yourself wearing a variety of hats. Those involved in the industry of Internet marketing are a hard working breed by nature and are typically not afraid to roll up their sleeves and become involved in all aspects of their marketing campaigns.

From brainstorming to develop a niche to designing aesthetically appealing and well optimized websites and from writing scintillating website content and intriguing press releases to remaining active on industry message boards, Internet marketers do it all.

However, problems arise as the individuals become more successful. Their niche markets begin to thrive and increase in number and completing all of these different tasks for several different niches is no longer feasible. This is when it is important to know what aspects to outsource to other qualified individuals. This book will take a look at outsourcing both copywriting and website design.

Outsourcing these two elements to professionals enables the Internet marketer to retain control of crucial elements of the business such as creating new niches and promoting existing niches. These two components are the most critical and by retaining absolute control of these elements and overseeing other elements it is not likely the quality of the niche markets will be compromised by outsourcing.

Leave the Copywriting to the Professionals

The copywriting required for an Internet niche marketing campaign is one of the first elements which should be outsourced. The content you provide on your websites, as well as in press releases, sales letters and eBooks is likely the first impression potential clients get of your niche market. Logically, it stands to reason that your copy should be well written, concise, informative accurate, persuasive and search engine optimized. With so many requirements it is obvious this work should be completed by a professional copywriter.

The services of a quality copywriter, especially one skilled in search engine optimization (SEO), may be a significant expense with many copywriters charging close to $1.00 per word for optimized content and over 30 cents per word for content which is not optimized. However, those in the industry of Internet niche marketing realize the value of quality copy for their websites and are willing to pay these fees because they know they will be more than compensated by the success of their niche markets.

Let the Experts Design and Optimize your Website

We have already discussed how writers with SEO skills are a valuable commodity but it is also important to note that website designers who possess SEO skills are critical to the success of Internet niche marketing campaigns. SEO is so important because high search engine rankings can drive a great deal of traffic to a niche website.

Internet users constantly rely on search engines to find them the most useful information for particular search terms and as a result it is not likely these same users will visit websites buried on the third or fourth page of search results. More realistically, they will visit the first couple of links in the search results and find the answers they are seeking. This is why it is so important for those in the industry of niche marketing to invest in SEO.

Keyword density is one component of SEO which is usually handled by the copywriter. However, there are many other SEO strategies which can be incorporated into the design of a website to bolster rankings. Some of these strategies are careful selection of domain names and titles, use of META and ALT tags and clean website design which contains an easy to navigate sitemap. These are just a few of the most basic SEO strategies but techniques and strategies for SEO change regularly as search engines adjust their algorithms and industry professionals attempt new techniques to improve their rankings.

SEO is not a simple process and is basically a full time job. For these reasons hiring a website design firm with SEO capabilities is critical to the success of Internet niche markets.

Chapter 16: Outsourcing: Getting the Job Done the Cheap Way

In today's world, being competitive will mean getting what you want in life and achieving your goals. This is also true in the business world where companies are now struggling to be on top of other companies in order to get their company to be the number one in the business that customers will choose.

However, because of the recent decline in the economy, companies today can no longer depend on themselves. They need help in order to make their companies competitive. This is why companies today are now outsourcing their business process or at least some of their business process to other countries.

The outsourcing job is considered as one of the largest industries in developing countries today. Besides, with the opportunity to earn lots of money, who wouldn't want to be in the outsourcing business?

Companies in the United State, Canada and European countries are now considering outsourcing their business process or at least some of the business process to developing countries, such as India, Philippines, China and Mexico. This is because labour rates in these developing countries are considered to be cheaper than doing it in-house.

For example, in the software development industry,

the company will have to hire talented IT professionals in order to get the job done. If they hire their own IT professionals, they will pay them a very high professional fee to develop the software. However, when they outsource it to IT companies in other countries who accept outsourced jobs, you will see that their equally talented IT professionals will do the job at a fraction of the price you have to pay in your country. Not to mention the full company benefits that you have to give to your IT professional.

Here is a detailed example on how it works in order to get a clearer picture. If an IT professional in your country will charge 500 hundred pounds for a project and you need at least one thousand of those projects, you will be spending five hundred thousand pounds to get it done. However, if you outsource it, you can expect that the equally talented IT professional in that country will only charge a fraction of the cost. They will only charge about 100 pounds per project. So, if you need one thousand projects done, you will only spend 100 thousand pounds to get all the projects done if you outsource it. More or less, you will be saving 400 thousand dollars to get the job done. And, this is a significantly large amount of money.

Another benefit that you can get from outsourcing is that you can divide your company's heavy workload. Because of this, your company will be able to focus more on important matters. Outsourcing can free your company and let it expand to a higher level.

There are other benefits that you can take advantage of in outsourcing. Not only can you save a lot of money in operational costs, and make time for your company to tackle on more important things but you can also make your company grow because you will be satisfying a lot more clients.

With outsourcing, you will be able to save lots of money and your company will fully use its resources by freeing it from less important jobs and let it focus more on very important projects. Just make sure that the company you plan on outsourcing your business process to can get it done on time and get it done right. By making sure of the quality, you will be satisfying your clients.

Chapter 17: Business Process Outsourcing: A Cheap Alternative to Get the Job Done

Try to imagine that you need a business process to be finished. You hire a professional in your country that charges about five hundred pounds to get the job done. This can prove to be too expensive for your company. What if you can get the job done, with the same quality made by a person with the same qualifications as the person you hired before, to do the particular business process at half the price?

This can prove to be very attractive. However, how can you be able to find this person with the same qualification but charges half the price your professional charges? The answer to this question is to outsource your business process in developing countries full of talented professionals.

Since developing countries have lower minimum salary rates, outsourcing can prove to be a cheaper alternative to do a particular business process that you need. Not only that, if your company is burdened with heavy workloads, outsourcing can help your company ease the burden. This will mean more efficiency and productivity for your company while saving a lot of money in the process.

By outsourcing your business process, you can be sure that you will be able to get the job done at half the price. Developing countries, such as India, China, Philippines, and others can provide cheap labour compared to hiring professionals in the United States or Europe.

Outsourcing companies is considered as a major industry in developing countries. Governments of developing countries are welcoming outsourcing companies to provide top quality jobs for their professionals with high paying salary. Although the salary you will give to outsourcing companies in other countries may be considered high, in the United States or Europe it will be considered to be very low, the minimum wage in developing countries is far lower than you can imagine.

Outsourcing business processes in other countries will also mean saving a lot of money on company insurance, social security payments and other benefits that you will be required to pay for if you hire a regular employee in your company to do the job.

As you can see, outsourcing your business process' main advantage is providing your company with cheap labour and at the same time quality and professionally done jobs. The bottom line for outsourcing is saving a lot of money for your company.

So, if you are looking for a way to get cheap labour for your company, you can consider looking outside your country for outsourcing companies that can tailor your needs for your company.

However, before hiring a particular outsourcing company, you have to make sure that the quality of their work meets your company's standards. Outsourcing companies are now providing ways for you to evaluate their work first before you hire them. Because of this, you can be sure that you will be getting the best outsourcing company to get your business process done.

Outsourcing doesn't only provide cheap labour for your company, but it can also ease the burden of heavy workload because of the growing demand for your company's services. Through outsourcing, you will be able to increase productivity and efficiency of your company.

However, you should always remember that outsourcing is not for everybody. You have to determine if your company should outsource your business process or not. If you think your company can handle it, you should keep the work in your company. But if it proves to be very burdensome, you should consider outsourcing. So, instead of hiring additional regular employees in your company, you can outsource your business process and save a lot of money.

Chapter 18: Business Outsourcing for Risk Management

When you hire a business outsourcing company for your risk management needs, you need to spell out the context for your risk management process.

The steps should include identification, planning, mapping, defining, developing, and mitigation.

A business outsourcing group is your best option for risk management issues. This is because if something happens you can put the blame on someone else and it is not all on you.

The first step the company will cover is identifying the risks that may occur to the company or the domain of interest.

You will need to establish a plan with the company for the remainder of the process for your risk management.

When you are working with a business outsourcing company they will map out the social scope of managing risk, the stake holder's objectives and identity, and the basis risks are evaluated.

They will also determine if there are any constraints that might slow down your project for establishing a good risk management process.

You will then need to establish a framework which will explain an agenda for all activities you need to complete to meet your goals. This will be a process of setting certain timelines for completions of certain projects.

Once you have worked with your business outsourcing group with these steps you will then need to develop an analysis plan to verify your risk management solution is successful. You will need to mitigate also using the resources available to you.

A business outsourcing company will help you with all of your needs when you need to establish a solid risk management plan for your business.

Chapter 19: Business Outsourcing Labour Criticism Issues

Many people believe business outsourcing to companies outside of the United States or UK is not right and we should hire our own citizens.

Many of the accusations are regarding keeping the money in the U.S/UK, dodging taxes, and more.

When a company uses business outsourcing for their project needs, customer or technical support, or call centres they are saving a lot of money they would normally have to pay to the government in taxes.

Businesses usually have to pay a double tax. Corporations are taxed on an extremely high level income tax rate. When a company uses a business outsourcing company then they don't have to pay the taxes to the United States or UK Government.

In addition, they are able to pay a much lower wage to people who are willing to accept whatever they can get. This can save a business millions of dollars in a year.

Another big criticism is that American and UK companies need to keep the money in the United States and UK. They need to create the jobs at home.

The money and the jobs should stay in the at home

and this would be supporting the local economy. Many people believe this argument to be true but the money savings is the biggest benefit.

Many people complain about companies outsourcing their employees and giving jobs to people outside of the United States and UK.

However, businesses benefit much more because of the high taxations that occur on businesses and the strict policies toward businesses.

Chapter 20: Business Process Outsourcing in Action

Business process is the skeleton of a certain business activity. It involves the description of different tasks and possible outcomes that are associated with a specific business activity. It is essential in crafting the business goals of a certain corporate organization, which is clearly defined in the organization's business strategy.

Business process is classified into three categories, which are as follows:

1. The management processes, which is followed to run the operation of the business and comply with all existing yet relevant requirements.

2. The operational processes, which is followed in delivering the business value to clients, and is considered as an integral part of a corporate organization's core business.

3. The supporting processes, which is followed to support the core-based processes. It includes accounting, information technology (IT) support, and recruitment processes.

Being the skeleton of your organization's business activity, you must give utmost importance to your business process as a whole. This is extremely important since the success or failure in achieving the goals of your business will largely depend on the process that you have followed, together with your business strategies and plans. Thus, without an effective business process, your business is as good as dead when the time comes.

Realizing the importance of a business process in achieving their business objectives, there are companies that prefer to outsource some or all of their business process (most specifically the non-core processes) to third-party organizations. The main motive in outsourcing a business process is to allow the business to invest most of their time, financial, and human resources into core activities and focus on building effective strategies, which will fuel the growth of the company.

Since the global marketplace is fast-changing and highly-competitive, your business must concentrate on improving the productivity and at the same time trim down unnecessary costs. Non-core business processes are being outsourced since the tasks involved in these processes consumes time, essential resources, and energy. Thus, outsourcing these non-core business processes will help you achieve a cost-efficient system.

Non-core business processes that can be outsourced range from production to customer service to support functions (such as software development). Most companies that are outsourcing their business process are from Western countries and they are delegating the work to outsourcing firms located offshore, especially countries located on the Eastern hemisphere, such as China, Philippines, India, and Malaysia.

While more and more companies are becoming comfortable with outsourcing their business processes, outsourcing most of their learning and development functions is still a new approach to many learning professionals. Moving the training and learning model that is completely in-house to one that will be handled by other individuals outside the business is a big leap. However, as mentioned earlier, it is important that these processes receive equal importance and consideration for the benefit of your business as a whole. Thus, despite of business process outsourcing as a new approach, many training and learning professionals are starting to get the grip of the new system and subsequently will follow the outsourcing trend.

Business process, especially the non-core one, needs to be given equal importance and attention to achieve an efficient business operation. Outsourcing these business processes will not be a waste of time and financial resources, but rather a strategy to be followed. Surviving in this highly-competitive global marketplace is not as easy as you think. You need an option that will work to your advantage — and that is outsourcing.

Chapter 21: Business Outsourcing Contracts

When you consider business outsourcing it is important to draw up a contractual agreement for you and the outsourcing company to sign.

This agreement will define the project in full including items such as the time line, budget, people, and more.

When you decide on a business for outsourcing it is important to draw up a contract. The contract will spell out all of your expectations to the project and what the role of the company and their employees will be.

This gives you the opportunity to hold the company accountable for the work you are asking to be done.

When you sign a contractual agreement for business outsourcing the contract will specify the time frame of the project and set a timeline.

The timeline will set milestones during the project and specify each with an expected completion date. In addition, many contractual agreements will specify percentages of payment according to the completion of each set milestone.

If the completion or the milestone is not met on the expected date, a stipulation may be defined on the contractual agreement also.

The contract signed between you and a business outsourcing company will define the budget of the project and what the company has agreed to do the project for.

If the company has underbid the project, then they must pay the excess funds to complete the project. It is not your responsibility if the company underbids and the contract should be clear on this.

This includes the amount of hours it takes for completion of the project. If the company promised the project would be completed in a certain amount of hours and it is not then their staff will be working for free until the project is completed.

You must sign a contractual agreement along with the business outsourcing company you are hiring. This is to protect the company and the funds you have for the project.

Chapter 22: Outsourcing your Business Process to China

China is the most populated country in the world filled with talented and skilled workers. It is also a place plagued with unemployment and poverty. This is why China is now entering the world of outsourcing where they can make use of their high population level and talented individuals.

Outsourcing is utilized by many companies in developed nations to save money on business processes. It is used by many companies because of the possibility to increase productivity and at the same time save a lot of money in terms of salary. Outsourcing from another country, particularly developing countries, is very popular because of the cheap labour available.

China is one of those countries who have very cheap labour. Because of this, China became a premier destination for businesses to hire outsourcing companies. With a lot of talented and skilled workers, China is definitely the place where you should outsource your business process. This is a great way to save a lot of money and at the same time, increase productivity with the same quality that talented individuals in your country is able to achieve.

For example, a talented professional in your country can do a certain job for you for a hundred pounds. However, if you outsource the same job to China, a worker with the same talent and skill as the professional in your country can get the job done with the same quality for only twenty pounds. You can clearly see how much you can save in outsourcing instead of hiring regular employees in your business.

Now, try to imagine that you need maybe 1,000 of those jobs done. If you will have it made locally with your own professional, it would cost you £100,000 to get all those 1,000 jobs done. However, if you outsource those 1,000 jobs to china, you will only spend £20,000 with the same quality. You will save £80,000 just to get the job done.

You see how beneficial outsourcing can be to your company. This is why you should consider outsourcing part of your business process to another country, such as China in order to make more profit and decrease heavy workloads to manageable pieces.

However, before you consider outsourcing part of your business process to China, you should consider the fact that not all outsourcing companies offer good quality services. You have to make sure that the particular outsourcing company offers good quality products and services and hires certified professionals to provide that quality.

You also have to consider the outsourcing company you plan on hiring about the history of their previous outsourcing jobs. It is recommended that the company should have enough experience in handling the business process you plan on outsourcing before.

Check out their previous clients and find out if there are companies that hired the outsourcing company with the same jobs that you plan on outsourcing. If they have, it is recommended that you should take a look at their jobs and determine if it is at par with your standards.

It is also important that once you hired a particular outsourcing company in China, you have to regularly check the job quality in order to determine if the quality is deteriorating or improving.

These are some of the things you should look for in an outsourcing company in China in order to make sure that you will get your money's worth. So, if you need to save money and at the same time, break down heavy workloads to manageable pieces, you should consider outsourcing in China.

Chapter 23: An Overview of Manufacturing Outsourcing

The on-going growth of the outsourcing industry is not an entirely new trend. As a matter of fact, it has been gradually increasing in size and number for several years now. Prior to the release of countless IT innovations, companies in urbanized countries have been accustomed to the term and practice of manufacturing outsourcing. They usually outsource manufacturing jobs to other developing nations nearby.

As a general rule, the system involves the outsourcing of jobs related to the manufacturing industry. A good number of companies also wind up building their own factory outlets out of the country, where the production materials are typically cheaper and labour costs are considerably lower. Canada, South Africa and Mexico are some of the countries that embrace this type of industry.

Manufacturing Outsourcing vs IT Outsourcing

Despite the numerous resemblances in terms, manufacturing and information technology outsourcing are two different areas of interest in the sense that they vary significantly in their relative pace and the additional overheads involved.

Manufacturing outsourcing was a fairly sluggish process that entailed the shifting of manufactured merchandise from the factory outlets in developing nations to their final destination. This scheme led to numerous job openings, especially in the transport sector. On the other hand, the IT sourcing industry failed to give rise to further work opportunities. This is mainly because of the fact that information is routinely exchanged by means of computers.

Manufacturing Outsourcing: the Products

The mass production of clothes and other garments in various Asian countries is a clear-cut example of manufacturing outsourcing. Companies from the United States and UK typically outsource the manufacture of goods in nations that offer lower production costs.

Microchips and other electronic parts are also candidates of manufacturing outsourcing. Giant electronic firms typically set up their own factories complete with the necessary technology needed for the production, as well as the packaging, of their goods.

Aside from the usual ready-to-wear apparels and microprocessors, the manufacturing industry also outsources various types of goods. One of which is the production of biomedical merchandise. As a matter of fact, it has become a widespread practice in numerous biotech firms, both big and small.

Outsourcing a wide array of tasks like regulatory filing, pre-clinical testing, and molecular genetics makes it possible for bigger companies to concentrate on their main transactions. In addition, it allows smaller firms to cut back on production processes that they are not well equipped to carry out.

One such operation may include the creation of innovative drugs intended for clinical trials, which entails putting together a suitable facility. Needless to say, the monetary risk is notably great considering the fact that FDA approval has not been obtained yet.

As biotech firms take contractual or full-time consultants into service to supervise outsourcing operations and handle communications, the pervasiveness of manufacturing outsourcing has indeed created a new forte in the biomedical industry.

Coming across a highly regarded and dependable service provider necessitates the need to take a number of things into account. Aside from the expected overheads, concerns that surround the management of proprietary information, manufacturer site, contract validity, quality monitoring, level of outsourcing, communication issues and data storage should also be considered.

Indeed, an eclectic array of products could easily fall under the wide umbrella of manufacturing outsourcing, given that certain conditions are fulfilled. Then again, company owners need to view the issue from all corners so as to ensure that the advantages are far greater than the cons; otherwise, the losses could also be as enormous as the prospective gain.

Chapter 24: Data Entry Outsourcing: Where to Find the Most Competent and Affordable Outsourcing Company

As an owner of a company or a business, you want to save money as much as possible in order to profit more and let your company grow. Thanks to the internet, outsourcing your business process can be done in other countries where qualified, and experienced computer operators are widely available at a very low cost.

Countries such as India, Philippines, China and other developing countries are now accepting outsourcing as part of a very lucrative industry.

Data entry work is one such thing that businesses and companies today are outsourcing to lighten the heavy workload and also to do it more efficiently, faster, and more accurate.

First of all, before you consider this option, you have to know what data entry is all about. Data entry operations include data conversion, image and document processing, image enhancement, catalogue processing services, photo manipulation services and others.

Data entry is a constant need for some organization or companies that needs to document its daily activities. So, if you need data entry jobs, you should consider outsourcing it to other companies abroad that offer quality data entry jobs at a very affordable price.

There are a lot of benefits that you can take advantage of if you outsource your data entry jobs. One is that you will be able to have your data entry jobs done at a very affordable price; two is that you will be able to get it done professionally by competent people; and three is that you will be getting rid of this extra work in your company. Meaning that you will be effectively separating your company's work into manageable pieces.

Data entry is often used in medical billing and transcribing. It can be done by freelancers or an outsourcing company from other parts of the world. Over the past two decades, data entry companies and freelancers have been doing this work.

While it is true that data entry jobs can be done in-house, but there are certain jobs that should be done by experts rather than your staff. If you need a particularly large job in data outsourcing, it would take a lot of time and will require overtime for your staff if you do it in-house. However, if you outsource it, your company will function more normally and focus on more important work in your business.

So, if you have a time-consuming and expensive data entry jobs that your company needs to finish, you can consider outsourcing the data entry jobs to freelancers, or data entry companies that accepts outsourced jobs. For example, catalogue management can prove to be very time consuming and expensive. This will involve handling and maintaining paper catalogues. By outsourcing it, you will save a lot of money and still have time for your company's priority.

Data entry outsourcing will certainly change the way you run your company. It will let you save a lot of money, get the job done professionally, and it will allow you to effectively manage your company's priorities and workloads.

Always remember that before you hire a company or a freelancer to outsource your data entry jobs, you should first check the quality of their work and their work experience. It is recommended that they should have at least experience in the field of data entry jobs you will be outsourcing.

Chapter 25: Data Outsourcing

The rapidly increasing market has caused an imperative need to come across beyond the traditional coverage of business. Conventional strategies have been cropped up. With these revolutionized methods, several companies have been swamped with data that takes a good length of processing time. As a measure for optimizing time data outsourcing has become a trend.

Principle of the Practice

This serves as a means where in companies could increase their sales immensely while at the same time allotting a less for labour expenses. In fact, it is a great solution for companies to sell various domestic products to a larger market range reaching even the most distant consumers. Through this an approximate of 35% to 40% overhead savings has taken effect.

The essential elements for data outsourcing are open communication, strong business relationship, and ongoing management. Software houses, outside consultancy, or service agencies are being contracted to handle the company's data bank through the performance of systems analyses, operations of data centres, and programming. Basically, this principle is especially rooted from the necessity of hiring qualified computer machinist at a considerable lower cost. Scope of Practice

More often than not, the data being outsourced are

those that generally consume a relatively longer time of handling. Outsourcing of data entry operations encompasses conversion of data, processing of documents, and catalogue development services. Image processing is also one area being outsourced through the manipulation and editing of photos.

Catalogue management involves the conversion of traditional paper based type into online, digital ones. Production cost for the latter type is lower than that of the former. The expense is largely spent on paper handling and maintenance. In addition to that a big chunk of time is needed to come up with the output.

With the technologically advanced kind, necessary changes and updates can easily be made and in a lesser amount of time. Technically, all that is needed is to click a button once data entry has been accomplished.

An accumulation of data is an influential management resource. Through the availability of low cost data entry outsourcing, there is an underlying possibility that the amassed information could be to be depleted and be better used and applied by the company. With this there is a constant need for data entry especially for those organizations that are doing day to day decision making.

In cases like this a regular and continuous data entry and processing is required. The necessity for data that could easily be accessible, accurate, and up to date is preferred by everyone.

The common types of enterprises employing and taking advantage of this means are mostly financial institutions, hospitals, pharmaceutical companies, publishing houses, law firms and court houses, oil companies, transportation companies, and even Ivy League universities.

Benefits

This new trend in business that makes use of outsourcing agencies, advantages goes more than the company in need of the services. Mostly, these companies are founded in first world or industrialized countries. Through this, third world or developing countries benefit with the mass employment being provided by outsourcing.

With the relatively easy to practice principles more people are given the opportunity to become contributory members of society. In addition to that, the countries where most agencies are located receive a larger sum of money from taxes and revenue.

The world of business has become localized in terms of being a global community working together to come up with a much better output.

Chapter 26: Outsourcing Data Entry Work

In the fast developing business world, most companies either big or small find it difficult to handle the large volumes of complex data. They need to spend more time, money and man power in data entry processing work. This situation calls for data entry outsourcing.

Outsourcing the data entry works to some other company would relieve them from the pressure of managing data entry jobs and they can spend the time and man power in some other useful tasks like improving the quality of product, customer service and so on. Outsourcing data entry works is also cost effective.

Data entry outsourcing is the best option for all the business requirements that need advanced data entry skills and tools. The data entry processing companies normally have large number of skilled personnel who accomplish any of the data entry processing tasks outsourced by the client company.

They deliver the final output as per the required format. Since the data entry processing company itself gives training and office supplies, the client companies relieve from the stress of training the employees and providing equipments to accomplish the data entry processing tasks.

Data entry outsourcing also helps the companies to get the uninterrupted supply of final output 24/7 365 days. Hence the companies can outsource any number of assignments and can get the error free, accurate output within the specified time limit.

Any type of data entry processing works can be outsourced like legal documents, manuals, payroll, questionnaire, books, research papers, bills, tax forms, customer survey forms, medical billing, records, memos, financial statements, product registration forms and much more.

Since the data entry processing companies have security measures like double keying process which involves re keying the data in different files which are then compared electronically with each other to provide accurate results to the client companies. Therefore selecting a genuine company for data entry outsourcing would help the companies get relief from most of the data processing problems.

There are some versatile data entry processing companies that can help the client company's data entry projects irrespective of the language and type. In fact versatility in addressing data entry projects is one of the main reasons for outsourcing data entry projects. The client companies can also get the output in desired format like via internet, FTP, CD-R, CD-RW and so on.

Data entry processing companies have skilled staffs that have up to date technologies in data entry field. Therefore outsourcing the job to them help you get the service done by latest technologies. These companies also have high speed scanners to transfer image files to readable format and so any type of projects can be allotted to them.

Outsourcing the data entry processing works to developing countries is becoming common nowadays. This helps get the desired output for comparatively less amount. However cost effectiveness do not generally mean lack of high standards. You would get the complete accurate data entry output at the specified time.

Hence choosing a reliable company to outsource data entry processing works provides a solution to all your information processing needs and so you can focus your attention on other business development processes.

Chapter 27: Your Options in Sales Force Outsourcing

Sales force outsourcing is not a new idea. It has been a dwelling practice in small and big businesses alike. Sales agents, distributors and resellers are the most common set ups in sales force outsourcing.

This industry however has been threatened with the rapid rise of BPO (Business Process Outsourcing) forcing Sales Force Outsourcing to be strategic alternative to indirect channels and sales agents.

Two Models of Sales Force Outsourcing

There are two models of sales force outsourcing: sales agents & distributors / resellers and BPO solution of Sales Force Outsourcing.

Sales Agents

A sales agent is someone who is self-employed and is the person who sells products on behalf of a company. Most often than not, the terms of payment is on commission basis though there are instances where a sales agent has basic salary. When delving into retail or manufacturing, sales agents usually carry multiple products and have established contacts. One may think that sales force outsourcing is a good option as solution. Yes it is a viable solution but this too has its own limitations.

The specialization of sales agents is based on a defined market that depends on the geography or the industry of a particular sector. They will only go for products that are sellable to their available contacts. This means that if you outsource your product to an existing market that has no interest for it, sales force outsourcing is not a good solution.

Another limitation of sales force outsourcing is for you to be able to have a larger coverage, you will need a number of sales agents that will need dedicated management resources to optimize your outsourced sales force.

Distributors / Resellers

Another option that may prove to be a good a solution for sales force outsourcing is through an indirect channel network. The important aspect when talking about distributors and sellers is that they own customer thus living up to the name "indirect sales channel." This aspect is also the difference between sales agents and distributors / resellers.

While a sales agent sells products for you or your company, distributors / sellers on the other hand buy your products and sell them to their customers. With this, you drop control over the end customer as well as being able to sell other services and products directly.

Just as the same with sales agent, it is limited to a point wherein you can only sell to those who have customers that are interested with your products.

Otherwise, sales force outsourcing through distributors / resellers will be a lost cost. That is why you need to choose carefully whom you partner up with - always research, research and research.

Sales Force Outsourcing Organizations

In the past, companies build an in-house direct sales force. The process in doing so requires a large amount of capital as well as expertise. Hiring, training and managing this kind of set up will put holes in the pockets of companies.

But if this kind of setup costs a lot of money, why do organizations opt for this? The answer: control. When sales agents or distributors / resellers sell your products, you have little to no control on what they do or how they sell your product.

Having an in-house sales force, a company will be able to have control over its markets, prices as well as choice of customers. This setup can be a competitive edge over other companies in the same industry.

As of today however, the business process outsourcing (BPO) sector is on the rise and because of this sales force outsourcing is becoming an alternative to having an in-house sales force. Unlike with utilizing sales agents and distributors / resellers, you still have control over the target markets, sales activity, and pricing.

It is like having an in-house sales force without having to shell out much capital money.

Chapter 28: Outsourcing India

Everyday the economies of the world are become more and more interdependent. Businesses all over the globe have gone through a lot of changes over the last few years. The rise of the information superhighway has paved a path for the outsourcing industry to grow. Through this, more and more business processes are being outsourced to destinations beyond the national domain of the main companies. The effectiveness of outsourcing as part of a business model has proven to be feasible and is directly related to growth and productivity.

Why India

Productivity and growth can somewhat be called the teaser benefits of outsourcing and the country at the number one spot that provides these two is India. All over the United States and the United Kingdom, India is the preferred destination for outsourcing assignments. In recent researches, forty four percent of the world's offshore outsourcing back office and software services are in India. It has also been noted that as many as 400 of the Fortune 500 companies have their own branches in India or are outsourcing to India utilizing Indian technology companies.

Why India? What makes India such a hot spot for outsourcing jobs?

There are several answers to these questions? One, India has a myriad of skilled people that are very available in the country. Because of this vast number, India can afford to trim down the cost of services without having to cut down on quality. Just by looking at the list of companies that have back office operations in India one will truly understand and believe this.

Airlines such as Lufthansa and British Airways outsource their ticket reservation in India. HSBC and GE outsource accounting in India. Dell and Microsoft outsource research work in India. Standard Chartered has its full back office operations for its global business in India.

Backed up with this kind of credentials, outsourcing organizations in India have developed systems to scale operations or to be able to handle in a professional manner the needs of the clients. The highly skilled work force in India provides not only high quality service but also other added services that are very valuable. An added advantage, which puts India on top of the list, is the ability of the people to speak in English.

It boasts of being the 2nd largest nation to have the most number of English speaking citizens thus companies based in the United States or the United Kingdom opt for outsourcing in India.

Another reason why India is an outsourcing hot spot is because of its government policies. Because of the support it gives to the outsourcing industry in the country, the government and its policies have ensured the growth of outsourcing in India. As of today, its value as an outsourcing destination has reached high status.

The stable democracy that India has been experiencing for the last six decades gives India an advantage in the outsourcing industry. The country's GDP rate of 9.2 percent, ever improving infrastructure and its status as a country that provides high quality of service, and rapidly developing technology makes it a hot spot destination for outsourcing.

Businesses all over the world have seen the benefits of outsourcing. They have now realized that outsourcing is not just an option for survival but a tool that when used properly, will greatly benefit their businesses. And with India showing much talent and skills, have become the favourite place of these businesses as an outsourcing destination.

Chapter 29: Payroll Outsourcing Services: Is it Right for your Business?

A lot of companies have been questioning if payroll outsourcing services is right for their business. Firstly, you have to know about payroll outsourcing before you try and hire an outsourcing company to do the payroll for you.

First of all, you first have to know what payroll outsourcing is. Payroll outsourcing services are outsourcing companies that will calculate your company's payroll, print and deliver checks to your company, adhere to the latest tax obligations, and also provide management reports.

So, why not just hire your own controller and manage your company's payroll? Why hire a payroll outsourcing company to do this for you?

There are so many factors that you should consider on why you should hire payroll outsourcing services for your company. First of all, if your company is rather large, it will be recommended that you should hire a company that offers payroll outsourcing services.

The first thing you have to ask yourself is if either you can handle all the calculations and details of your payroll with precision, on time, and accurate. If you are not confident making the payroll, you will need to hire a company that offers payroll outsourcing services.

The second thing you have to consider is the size of your company. Since making a payroll means that you have to make individual computations for your employees, a company that has a particularly large numbers of employees (more than 20 people) will need to hire a payroll outsourcing services. Besides, you don't want to burden yourself with computing the amount that each of your employees will receive.

You also have to understand all of the details involved in a filing your payroll taxes as a company and for each of your employees. If you don't understand the details, you better get payroll outsourcing services. You do not want to get in to trouble related to taxes and you definitely do not want yourself and your company be investigated by the IRS in the US, Inland Revenue in the UK.

Payrolls are what employees look forward to every month. If you cannot handle making the payroll on time, it is wise that you should hire a payroll outsourcing company. You definitely do not want a group of disgruntled employees outside your door asking when their paycheques will arrive. By hiring a payroll outsourcing company, you can be sure that you and your employee's paycheques will arrive on time.

By outsourcing your payroll, you will be sure that the computations will be precise, accurate and on time. You will never have to worry about late payments for your employee and never worry about computation problems again that may get you into trouble.

There are a lot of payroll outsourcing companies offering their services today. You have to choose a company that offers great quality in their work and offers it at a very reasonable price. It is also important that the company should provide maximum security in dealings.

These are some of the reasons on why you should hire a payroll outsourcing services. With this, you will be able to focus more on your role in the company and you will also be confident that the payroll you will have will be precise, on time and accurate. So, if you have a particularly large company, and you do not understand how a payroll works, you should consider hiring a payroll outsourcing services.

Chapter 30: Improve Sales by Outsourcing Call Centres

Outsourcing call centres are excellent methods of generating sales and help current customers with technical support and customer support issues for several small, medium and large businesses.

Some larger companies have the time, resources and money to put in place their own call centres but most smaller and medium-sized businesses opt for a streamline approach to call centres and choose to outsource the needs of their call centres.

Helpful Tips on Outsourcing Call Centres

First off, if you are searching on ways to outsource a call centre, the business have to first decide on what they are trying to achieve in the course of action.

Most businesses are looking for low cost methods to either sell goods or provide support for customers. The reason why most businesses choose to outsource call centres is generally due to the low cost.

On the business side, outsourcing call centres takes careful decision making and analysis, as well as discussion and result on the outsourcing side.

For example, even before a business makes a decision to deal with a call centre with an outsourcing firm, it must first see its business needs and comprehend how the new service will either generate sales or enhance customer satisfaction, thus developing customer retention and limiting customer churn.

In case the business realizes what kinds of services it requires, the business normally bids from call centre outsource services. The bidding process removes several of the contractors that cannot meet the qualifications, labour and technological requirements of the business.

Once a call centre is contracted for services with a business, a deeper consultation takes place wherein the business and the outsource work together in order to create a solution that can either generate sales for services or products or provide customers with support for technical or billing products.

There are several call centre outsourcing companies available and as a business seeking solutions, it is your job to contract with one of them and choose the one that can deliver results you desire.

Since each outsource call centre company offer a different product, the best option is to analyze the specific needs and perform plenty of researches to locate a match with a company that can fulfil the business's needs.

How to Reduce Turnovers and Retain Manpower

A turnover or churn normally reflects the percentage of customer service representatives that leave a call centre in a specified period. This is the most common problem of call centres.

Additionally, this factor plays a role in reducing the quality, increasing recruitment and training costs, and reducing the marketability of a call centre operation.

In order to reduce turnovers, appropriate planning and tracking and figuring out the main cause of the event is necessary. You can start by hiring the right people. This can be done by developing a profile of the team members that have been with the company for some time and are happy and productive. Always look for characteristics that can match that profile whenever assessing new applicants.

Improving the line managers is also a good help. Train line managers on how to supervise his or her team members for attaining superior productivity. Teach them that they can manage without being controlling or critical. Honing their soft skills, monitoring performance and rewarding them for enhanced productivity can usually diminish high turnover rates.

Chapter 31: Outsourcing Everything Except the Profit

When it comes to outsourcing, there is no doubt about the fact that the most beneficial advantage is the ability to reduce costs by outsourcing tasks and projects when appropriate. Some Internet marketers take the concept of outsourcing to the extreme by outsourcing the majority of their niche marketing tasks. In other industries this strategy could lead to imminent failure because the client may lose control of the project. However, when it comes to Internet niche marketing this strategy can be very effective and result in the marketer have a greatly reduced workload and a substantially larger profit margin.

Why Outsourcing Almost Everything Works

In the Internet niche marketing industry, outsourcing almost all of the required tasks can be a profitable strategy. Some of these tasks include copywriting, website design and website management. The marketer may chose to outsource all of these tasks and keep the most important tasks, namely niche selection and keyword development, to himself to ensure he remains in control of these critical elements.

Outsourcing Content Creation

Copywriting is one element of Internet niche marketing which can easily be outsourced. There is a plethora of talented writers with experience in writing copy for websites which is informative, interesting, accurate and also persuasive. There are many talented writers offering their services who are capable of creating this type of content. However, there is a much smaller pool of talented writers who are also skilled at the art of search engine optimization (SEO). These writers have the above mentioned skills but are also capable of weaving keywords into the articles in a way which appeals to both search engines and those reading the website.

Outsourcing Website Design

Similarly to the writing industry, there are countless website designers who are capable of creating high quality websites that are both aesthetically pleasing as well as functional. Again, there is a much smaller pool of website designers who have the capabilities of designing a website so that it is well optimized for search engines. SEO is critical to the success of any Internet niche marketing campaign because high search engine rankings improve website traffic. For this reason it is easy to understand why those with SEO skills are in such high demand. It is also easy to understand why those in the Internet marketing industry are willing to pay so much for these services.

Outsourcing Niche Website Management

Internet marketers who are balancing multiple niches have an even further opportunity to outsource even more of their responsibilities. They may find those skilled in the art of management to oversee a few of the niches. These managers will assume the responsibilities for organizing content for the website, and developing and maintaining the website design including the ongoing SEO effort for the website.

Special care should be taken when outsourcing management responsibilities. While it is important to verify the qualifications of copywriters and website designers and to search for highly qualified candidates, this is especially important when outsourcing tasks of a management nature. This is important because the tasks assigned to this individual can have a more dramatic impact on the niche market. If the manager fails to do an adequate job overseeing the assigned tasks, the niche may begin to wane in popularity. When this happens regaining the attention of audience members who were disappointed in changes occurring in the website can be extremely difficult.

Chapter 32: Raising the Bar Through Outsourcing

The stereotypes associated with outsourcing are often very negative in nature. However, it is actually possible to utilize the concept of outsourcing to receive the highest quality of work possible. Outsourcing no longer only refers to overseas sweatshops where employees work long hours for little pay. Outsourcing now also occurs domestically and often at prices which are more than generous. Thanks to savvy entrepreneurs who realize the benefits of offering their services on a contract basis, outsourcing has become the wave of the future. This book will take a look at how outsourcing can actually lead to superior work and increased profitability.

Top Quality Work from Industry Experts

One of the most advantageous aspects of outsourcing is the ability to employ industry experts for the completion of certain tasks. This becomes beneficial in situations where a business is faced with a complex problem which is beyond the expertise of the in-house employees. Outsourcing gives the business the opportunity to outsource the task of solving the problem to a highly qualified candidate. Although the business may pay a hefty sum for the individual's services this fee will likely be significantly less than what it would have cost them to solve the problem with their in-house staff. The amount of time it would have taken coupled with the potential for costly mistakes makes it clear outsourcing is the right decision in this scenario.

Another scenario where tasks may be outsourced to an industry expert is when the business is faced with the task of performing more work than they are capable of handling in-house. During aggressive deadlines or unexpected delays, outsourcing can be used to complete projects according to unyielding deadlines.

Flexibility in Scheduling

Many businesses balance the workload they take on based on the number of employees they have on staff capable of assisting in each individual task. However, outsourcing gives businesses the ability to consider accepting more work than their in-house employees are capable of completing. An example of when this is beneficial is when consultants are awarded more projects than they had anticipated and are suddenly in a situation where they are not able to meet their deadlines due to larger than anticipated workloads.

Another advantage to outsourcing is the ability to take on larger projects than usual. One of the most elementary factors often considered when awarding projects to consultants is the number of staff members who are available to work on the project. Clients evaluate this number with their project needs and schedule to determine whether or not they think the consultant is capable of completing the project on time. Consultants who outsource portions of their projects are effectively able to increase the amount of employees they can afford to have working on a particular project.

Reduced Operating Costs

Finally, outsourcing can help companies to produce higher quality work by enabling them to reduce their operating costs. Outsourcing can save companies a great deal of money because they often do not have to pay benefits such as social security, workers" compensation and Medicare to those who perform work on a contract basis. Additionally, those who perform the outsourced work typically do the work from their own office meaning the company does not have to provide resources for the individual. Although these costs may seem trivial, they can really add up especially if outsourcing is used on a regular basis.

Combined with the reduced operating costs, many companies find that productivity is increased through outsourcing. By outsourcing work to qualified individuals, the in-house employees are freed of additional responsibilities and can focus exclusively on the tasks they were hired to perform. This is significant because without outsourcing these same employees might be tasked with attempting to perform complicated tasks for which they are not properly trained or qualified. When this happens there is a significant decline in productivity as the employees take longer than necessary to complete the more complicated tasks and do not have time to complete the simpler tasks.

Chapter 33: Maintaining Quality of Service when Business Outsourcing

When you have poorly defined your contract with a business outsourcing company, the quality of the project may suffer severely.

There are many things you can do to verify the project maintains the expected quality when you are using a company other than yours.

When you define the objectives for the project you want completed they need to be defined clearly and everyone needs to acknowledge and sign off that they agree to them.

You should not forget anything.

Being too picky is better than not being specific enough. By forgetting certain things and not specifying them you are opening a door for poor work to be done.

When this happens, you cannot request it be changed and done a different way because it was not specified in the contract.

What will happen, is that you will have to pay additional money to have things done the way you want because you didn't properly specify in the contract.

One person should not write the specifications for the project. Projects need to be written by everyone who will be involved and affected by the project.

You need to be sure you don't miss anything that might cause poor quality with the project. If you need to research equipment and how things are properly done then you should.

Many people can be affected by poor quality in a project such as your employees who are using the equipment.

However, shareholders and stakeholders also have a vested interest that the money being spent on an outsourced project is spent well.

You don't want to be out of a job because you were not clear about how the project needed to be done and now you have a completed project but it makes your customers very unhappy.

Chapter 34: Communications Problems with Business Outsourcing

If you are looking to save money and thinking about using a business outsourcing company for your telemarketing or your technical support needs, you must consider the communication issues that might arise with outsourcing.

Many times when people call a customer service or call centre for assistance with their account information for a company they complain because there is a language barrier and it is hard to understand what the people are saying.

If you are considering hiring a company for your outsourcing needs, you should ensure that the customer service representative's first spoken language is of the customers who will be calling.

If it is not, it should be guaranteed to you that the representatives will be able to speak your language well enough to understand them.

One way to guarantee the language barrier will not exist with the customer service representatives from the outsourcing company you are hiring are for you and other team members to make phone calls to the representatives who will be representing you.

This way, you and your team members can speak to

the individuals and verify if their spoken language is good enough for your customers.

Most communications problems with call centres and customer service representatives occur from using offshore outsourcing groups.

Business outsourcing can save your company a lot of money. However, it is for you to decide which is more important, your customer satisfaction with your customer service and support or the amount of money you are saving through your outsourcing endeavours. You may find your customer count goes down once you begin outsourcing your customer service needs.

Chapter 35: The Benefits of Outsourcing in Small Businesses

Before we can begin discussing the benefits of outsourcing especially in small businesses we must fully understand what outsourcing is and what outsourcing is not (as many people often confuse it with off-shoring, a similar but different thing).

So what is outsourcing? A fairly recent addition to business terminology, outsourcing in a business is the delegation of certain non-core operations to other separate entities that specialize in those operations. Put very simply, outsourcing means giving away certain tasks which though imperative to the actual business, can be better managed by another industry which specializes in that task.

Outsourcing entails transferring management control and decision making power to the other industry as well. This means that there is a lot more interaction, and information exchange, coordination and trust between the outsourcer and its client, making it different from the established buyer-seller relationship.

Now that we have established what outsourcing is, let's focus on what it is not. Outsourcing is commonly confused to off shoring, which is the relocation of an entire or part of a functional unit of the business to another nation, whether it remain in that business's control or not. Outsourcing is usually limited

131

domestically. In many cases, such as telemarketing, the company wishes to employ the service of overseas call centres. Thus when outsourcing crosses national borders it is called offshore outsourcing.

So why should companies outsource? There are plenty of benefits of outsourcing, especially for small businesses. The main reason for outsourcing is the cut in costs, as they don't have to provide benefits to their workers, and have fewer overhead expenses to worry about. Many businesses prefer offshore outsourcing, as it allows them to utilize the low labour costs of countries such as India and China. Not only that, the relatively high exchange rates in these countries makes offshore outsourcing more advantageous.

Outsourcing also allows smaller businesses to focus on core competencies, and relieve themselves of the peripheral ones. Thus they can concentrate on providing better quality products and service. Even if the quality does not improve, the cut in cost allows for greater productivity. This increases the overall economy in total. Not just that, the business can produce good quality products without having to employ a large amount of people. Thus lowering their overall labour charges and employee benefit.

The best facet of outsourcing though is the ability to employ professionals to get the work done. In areas such as advertising and telemarketing, it is usually more cost effective, and productive to hand over the task to a separate company and pay them accordingly. Thus instead of handling their own affairs in a substandard manner, they can employ professionals to carry out the process efficiently and effectively. And once the outsourcing company is assured that its client is managing perfectly, it can focus on creating better products and services.

For small businesses, outsourcing allows them to work with the minimum of labour and equipment expenditure. For example, a small firm outside city limits can outsource its transport, thus making it unnecessary for it to acquire buses, cutting the cost of fuel and saving its resources. Another prime example is telemarketing and advertising. Many companies prefer to outsource this facet of marketing to professional call centres and advertising agencies, thus eliminating the need to form an entire unit devoted to this task. Not only that, but because the outsourcing client has a fully established infrastructure devoted especially to the service provided, there is no necessity for a small business to invest in developing its own internal infrastructure to accommodate that service.

In small businesses there is only a limited access to resources and ideas. Outsourcing allows the business to garner new ideas and innovations. It could also result possible cash influx due to the transfer of assets to the new provider.

Chapter 36: Reaping the Benefits of Outsourcing

Outsourcing was once the playground of big players in the economy. With the dawn of the Internet however, the smaller fishes have been given the chance and opportunity to take part in the outsourcing business. "But what is the big fuss about outsourcing anyway?" Outsourcing, in today's economy, can provide companies, big or small, benefits.

Cost Advantages

Cost advantages are one of the benefits of outsourcing. This can be done through outsourcing to other countries such as the Philippines and India. You can avail of services at a lower cost without sacrificing the quality since they also provide the same level of quality, sometimes even higher, to outsourcing services in the United States and UK.

Examples of the services that are usually outsourced in other countries are teleradiology, call centre services, and medical billing etc. By doing this, companies can cut down their costs to as high as one hundred percent when outsourcing. This is probably the best benefit companies can get when companies outsource.

Huge Amounts of Savings

Savings does not just pertain to money. When outsourcing, companies can also save on time, effort, manpower and infrastructure.

Time can be saved with outsourcing. Since you just assign specialized tasks to specific companies, there is no need to spend time on things such as planning and training people.

In outsourcing, companies do not have to invest in infrastructure thus there is no need to make a budget for any unneeded fixed investments. Also, the company does not have to maintain or change infrastructure.

When it comes to training costs, companies do not have to shell out money since there is no need to invest in manpower. There is no need to purchase new tools and equipment for specific jobs and functions.

Increase your Profits

Huge amounts of savings plus high quality work equals increase in profits. This is due to the fact that companies can give more focus on the core of the business rather than on the non-core aspect.

Outsourcing can increase profits especially if the outsourced company provides high quality service at a lower cost.

Increase Level of Efficiency

With the company focusing on the core of the business, results can be expected to be better. With non-core aspects of the business outsourced to other companies specializing in specific jobs, better results too are to be expected. This efficiency can provide the client company the efficiency it needs and even better.

Spreading the Risks

When different tasks are distributed through outsourcing, risks held by one person can be divided to several other groups. This also means that risks are lessened since tasks are given duly to people who specialize in them. If one group of people commits a mistake, the work of another group will not be in any way affected especially in terms of quality. Problems can also be easily fixed since the sources can be easily detected and pinpointed.

Providing Opportunity

This is not a benefit for the outsourcing client company but for the people who provide the service. Because of outsourcing, a lot of people were given the opportunity to have work. This is especially true to big companies in the United States and UK outsourcing in countries such as India and the Philippines.

This also proves that the benefits of outsourcing go two ways: for the client company and the companies who provide the services.

Chapter 37: The Risks in Offshore Outsourcing

Outsourcing, specifically offshore outsourcing is growing at a promising rate every year and shows no signs of slowing. Although some organizations have apprehensions on taking on this venture, it has not stopped the development of offshore outsourcing.

However, just like with anything else in the business world, there are always risks entailed with every endeavour and offshore outsourcing is not an exception. There are quite a few risks those organizations which, practice offshore outsourcing or those who are planning to, should know about.

Data Protection

Security practices differ from country to country that is why it is a must to check whether the vendors you have partner up with has the kind of protection and security practices that your company requires. When working on international business, the risk of security leakages is high. Although this is not really that much of a major concern in offshore outsourcing, data protection and security should be implemented as much as possible.

Cost-Reduction Expectations

Organizations automatically assume that they will be able to save a lot basing on a man-to-man comparison. This should not be the case since there are hidden costs that underlie in different offshore outsourcing models. Cost-reduction expectation should also take this into consideration. The cost savings in offshore outsourcing is gradual and does not happen in a short span of time.

Loss of Business Knowledge

There are some organizations that have business knowledge that is inherent only with the developers of applications. This knowledge could be a competitive advantage over other companies in the same industry. It should be carefully evaluated whether such knowledge base is to be outsourced or not since doing so entails the risk of losing this to other companies.

Failure of Vendor Organization to Deliver

It is important to always have a backup plan in case the vendor organization fails to deliver. This however rarely happens but it does and can happen. The client company should assess the different consequences if such thing should happen. Will it make a big impact on the company? What can the company actually do if it happens? Analyzing these risks is very crucial when offshore outsourcing.

Government Policies

When offshore outsourcing, you need to ensure that the vendor organization you have team up with follows the rules and regulations stipulated by the local government. Mostly, the issue of transparency is most important here.

Cultural Differences

Although some nations, such as India, are proficient in speaking the English language, there are still some noticeable differences such as in pronunciation, accents and diction.

Not just with language, there are certain cultural differences that could become problematic in the future. This includes difference in religions, the way of dressing and communication, the way and how messages are conveyed to superiors or underlings.

Knowledge Transfer

It takes time and a lot of effort to transfer knowledge from the client company to the vendor organization. It has been observed that during the initial stages of the agreement that there is a decline in productivity. This is due to the fact the most of the time during the initial stage is spent on transferring knowledge.

Different strategies may need to be implemented to increase the pace of knowledge transfer thus increasing the productivity level only in a short amount of time.

Chapter 38: Dangers of Business Outsourcing

Business outsourcing is becoming more and more popular each day. However, you need to be careful when you do decide to hire an outside company for your project.

Some of the problems that may occur are turnover, knowledge, and attitude problems. These can be difficult to handle.

When you hire a business outsourcing company to provide you staff on a temporary basis problems often occur with turnover rates.

Outsourcing companies have a higher turnover rate than most companies and you need to be prepared if you tend to go through employees quickly.

When turnover occurs you have to continue to train them. If you need to pull an employee from their current workload to train a new employee then this can create a problem with that employee getting behind.

Turnover can also cause problems with knowledge of the company. When you have to retrain employees about policies and procedures it might take some time for a new employee to get the hang of things.

Most employers believe it takes approximately two

weeks for a new employee to get settled in. However, your customer service may take a hit and you might have customers complaining about your service.

Another thing you need to think about with outsourcing is that the employee is not working for you. Many temporary employees want a full-time job with the company they are working for because they need the benefits.

However, when an employee is not really working for you then they do not take on the mission and the vision of the company and believe in instilling it.

Often times, you might see outsourced employees not care about the company like they should.

You should ensure all outsourced employees will hold true to the company although they are not really your employee.

Chapter 39: Is Educators Focus on Outsourcing Strategies, Open Source Technology

Many educational institutions offering IT curriculum are beginning to understand the importance of focusing on the administrative and managerial aspects of IT training. With outsourcing a regular occurrence in the industry and the popularity of open source technology on the rise, many colleges and universities have recently overhauled their IT programs to include additional curriculum related to these important facets of the IT world.

Outsourcing is a necessity for many businesses who are either not large enough to house a complete IT department or cannot find qualified individuals to hire for large scale, multilevel IT tasks, such as software installations, client server monitoring and local area or wide area network security.

The reason outsourcing has become such a major issue for many of these companies has to do with the quality of services rendered and the economic implications of not being familiar with the dollar value of the work performed. The problem of IT department managers outsourcing specific tasks as a means of avoiding having to gain at least a rudimentary understanding of them can have disastrous consequences on productivity and the bottom line.

Recognizing the need for training in the area of outsourcing has led many colleges and universities to promote outsourcing related coursework to a position of prominence in their overall administrative IT degree programs.

Open source technology can be a godsend for many industries yet almost always presents major problems for IT administrators, especially those who must monitor an environment where open source and commercial technologies coexist. Licensing issues and the tendency for open source programs to be modified extensively can wreak havoc on system fluidity and make the job of managing multiple platforms difficult.

Integration strategies for IT administrators are a type of training that many in the industry feel is long overdue. Educational institutions are beginning to see the need for such training and, although it is not yet covered as in-depth as outsourcing strategies, many have begun offering it as non-required curriculum.

Changes in the IT landscape are quick to find their way into educational programs that are currently producing the next generation of IT managers and administrators. In an industry that changes from week to week, it is become a necessity.

Chapter 40: Guide to Outsourcing

Those who are considering outsourcing portions of work for the first time may be feeling overwhelmed and hesitant about the concept of relying on someone outside the company to complete work related tasks. The discomfort with deciding whether or not to outsource work stems largely from ignorance about the process of outsourcing. This book also serve as a guide to those who are considering outsourcing for the first time and will provide information on how to select qualified candidates, establish project requirements and enforce a deadline for project completion.

Select Qualified Candidates Carefully

One way to greatly simplify the process of outsourcing is to give special consideration to selecting a qualified candidate to complete the outsourced tasks. This is important because outsourcing the project to an individual who is qualified to complete the tasks and motivated to do a good job will make the outsourcing endeavour more likely to be successful.

To find the right candidate for the job, place advertisements outlining the project requirements and preferences and carefully review each application which is submitted. Immediately disregard applicants who are not qualified for the position. Then review the applications of qualified candidates carefully and select a small group of the most promising candidates. Next interview each of these candidates and verify their references and passed work experiences to learn more about these candidates and their abilities and work ethics.

After interviewing these candidates it is time to make a decision regarding hiring one of the final candidates. Do not be discouraged if none of the final candidates seemed right for the job because you are under no obligation to hire any of them. You can continue your search for a qualified candidate by placing your job advertisement again and soliciting new responses.

Establish Definite Requirements

When outsourcing a project or tasks, it is important to clearly define the project requirements. This is critical because it is important for the contractor to fully understand the tasks which are being outsourced to ensure he is fulfilling all of the requirements and completing the task in a satisfactory manner.

Failure to establish definite project requirements and goals can lead to a great deal of problems when outsourcing a project. The contractor may feel as though he has completed the project as it was outlined but the employer may disagree. When this happens there can be harmful delays until the issues can be resolved amicably. In the case that this is not possible it might be necessary to employ the assistance of a mediator to evaluate the contract documents and the work produced to determine if the contract terms were met.

Establish a Firm Deadline

Another important element of outsourcing is establishing a firm deadline for the project. This is important to avoid misunderstandings and to prevent late submissions of work. Setting milestone goals is also important because it gives the employer the ability to evaluate the progress of the contractor during different stages of the project and to ensure it is proceeding according to schedule.

Ideally the deadline should be established before the candidate is chosen. This is important because this enables the employer to verify that the contractor is available for the duration of the project. Schedule should be discussed early in the process of selecting a candidate to avoid selecting an ideal candidate only to find out he is unavailable when his services are required.

Chapter 41: Conclusion

The business process involves a lot of things. It will involve every aspect of your company in order to let your company operate smoothly and efficiently. It will involve business tasks, such as marketing, payrolls, help desks, management, human resources and more.

In the past, handling all these can be easy. But because of the growing demands in businesses today, you have to consider that it will be difficult for your company to cope up with today's competitiveness in the business world. Your company should maximize its resources in order to remain competitive with other companies.

This would be impossible or very expensive if you handle every business process involved. This is why many companies are now considering outsourcing their business process.

Business process outsourcing is one of the most popular and the most cost-efficient business solution **that you can ever make**. By contracting other companies to do a specific business task, you will be taking off extra work involved in your company and focus more on important aspects in running your business.

For example, making payrolls can be time consuming. It will involve computation of salaries of every employees and it will also involve taxes. You can hire your own employees to do the payroll for you. But, this will only add to the expenses that your company is making. Your target would be to decrease overall expense in your company. So, in order to save money, you have to outsource this particular business process to companies that accepts outsourcing.

Another example would be the help desk. Every company that manufactures products needs one. This particular business process is a way to communicate with your clients and know about their feedback in your products and it is also a way to assist your clients in case they encounter difficulty with your product. Creating a help desk department may prove to be too costly. It will involve everything from hiring additional employees and purchasing all the necessary tools you need to create an efficient and working help desk.

Today, there are available call center companies that will be able to provide a help desk for you. They will be the one who will answer your calls and generate reports regarding each caller and providing the reports for your company.

Companies regularly outsource their business process offshore, particularly to developing countries filled with qualified and talented individuals, such as China, Philippines, Mexico and India. These countries offer good quality services for your business process and they charge a very cheap rate for these services.

By outsourcing your company's business process or some of your company's business process, your company will be able to utilize its facilities to its maximum potential.

Through business process outsourcing you will be able to cut some operational costs and at the same time, let your company focus more on important factors in running your own business.

These are the reasons why you should consider outsourcing your business process to offshore companies.

Always keep in mind that you should first check the quality of an offshore outsourcing company first before you sign the contract in order to be sure that you will be getting your money's worth. Remember this and it will pave the way to make your company the best in the industry.

Good Luck!